RESPIRATOR QUALITY AND SAFETY

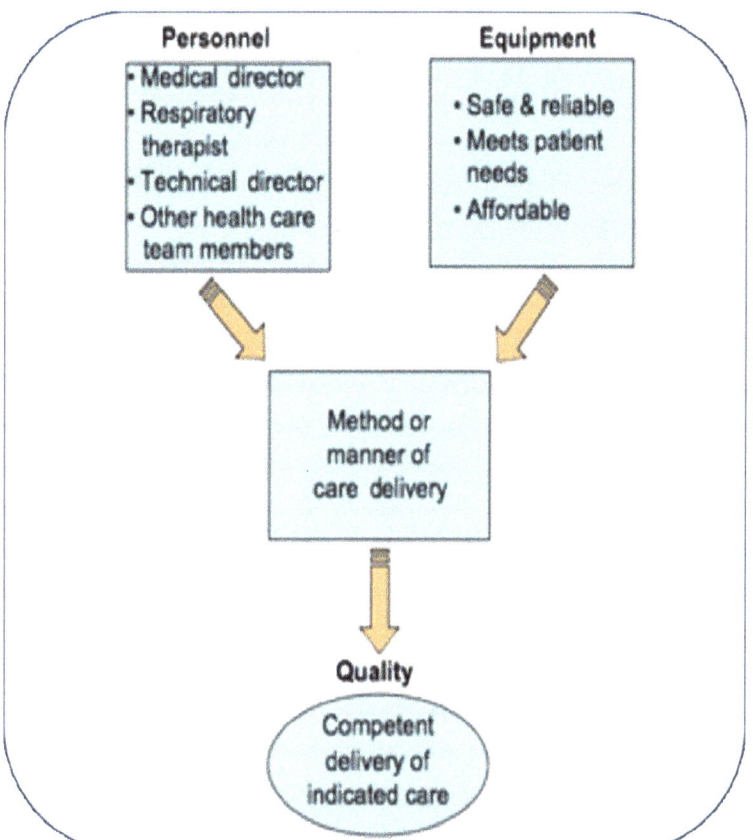

TABLE OF CONTENTS

INTRODUCTION 2

MODULE ONE 3

    LESSON ONE: THE FUNDAMENTALS OF RESPIRATORY CARE 3

    LESSON TWO: SAFETY PROTOCOLS IN RESPIRATORY CARE . 7

MODULE TWO 11

    LESSON ONE: QUALITY IMPROVEMENT IN RESPIRATORY CARE 11

    LESSON TWO: PATIENT ASSESSMENT AND MONITORING ... 16

MODULE THREE 21

    LESSON ONE: TECHNOLOGICAL ADVANCES IN RESPIRATORY CARE 21

    LESSON TWO: EMERGENCY MANAGEMENT IN RESPIRATORY CARE 26

MODULE FOUR... 30

    LESSON ONE: CHRONIC RESPIRATORY DISEASE MANAGEMENT 30

MODULE FIVE 34

    LESSON TWO: RESPIRATORY CARE IN SPECIAL POPULATIONS 34

MODULE SIX... 39

    LESSON ONE: ETHICAL AND LEGAL CONSIDERATIONS IN RESPIRATORY CARE... 39

MODULE SEVEN 44

    LESSON ONE: INNOVATIONS AND FUTURE DIRECTIONS IN RESPIRATORY CARE... 44

CONCLUSION 49

REFERENCES 50

COURSE OVERVIEW

This course is designed to equip healthcare providers with the knowledge and skills necessary to deliver high-quality, safe, and effective respiratory care. This course covers the fundamental principles of respiratory physiology and pathophysiology, advanced assessment and diagnostic techniques, therapeutic interventions, infection control, mechanical ventilation, and continuous quality improvement strategies.

COURSE OBJECTIVES

By the end of this course, participants will be able to understand Respiratory Care Quality and Safety, The Fundamentals of Respiratory Care, Safety Protocols in Respiratory Care, Quality Improvement in Respiratory Care, Patient Assessment and Monitoring, Technological Advances in Respiratory Care, Emergency Management in Respiratory Care, Future Trends and Continuing Education in Respiratory Care

COURSE MATERIALS

To learn this course, **healthcare providers/ participants** must be provided with materials like a Pen, pencil, notebook, and notepad to better understand and make it easy for them to learn.

INTRODUCTION

In today's fast-paced healthcare environment, the demand for high-quality respiratory care has never been greater. Respiratory care encompasses a broad range of services aimed at managing and improving the respiratory health of patients. It involves the assessment, treatment, and care of patients with acute and chronic respiratory conditions. As respiratory therapists and healthcare providers, our mission is to deliver care that is not only effective but also safe.

This book, "Respiratory Care Quality and Safety: A Comprehensive Guide for Healthcare Providers," is designed to serve as an informative and engaging resource for healthcare professionals committed to excellence in respiratory care. Whether you are a seasoned respiratory therapist, a nurse, a physician, or a healthcare student, this guide aims to provide you with a thorough understanding of the principles and practices that underpin high-quality and safe respiratory care.

Quality and safety are the cornerstones of effective healthcare delivery. Quality in respiratory care involves providing services that meet the highest standards and are evidence-based, efficient, and patient-centered. Safety, on the other hand, involves preventing harm to patients through the implementation of best practices, adherence to protocols, and continuous vigilance. This book is structured to provide a comprehensive exploration of these themes, starting with an introduction to the basic principles of respiratory care. It then delves into the specifics of safety protocols and quality improvement initiatives, which are essential for maintaining and enhancing the standard of care. Each lessson builds on the previous one, offering a cohesive narrative that links theoretical knowledge with practical application.

MODULE ONE

LESSON ONE: THE FUNDAMENTALS OF RESPIRATORY CARE

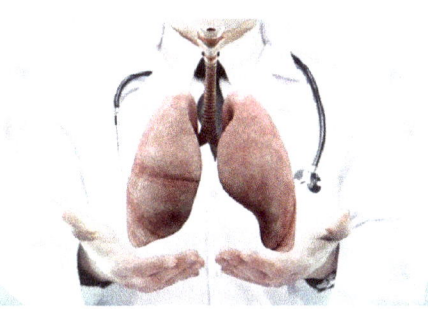

Respiratory care is a vital component of healthcare, focusing on the prevention, diagnosis, treatment, and management of patients with respiratory illnesses and diseases. This lesson provides a foundational understanding of respiratory care, outlining its history, key principles, and the essential skills required for effective practice.

The Evolution of Respiratory Care

The field of respiratory care has evolved significantly over the past century. Early forms of respiratory therapy can be traced back to the 1940s when the first inhalation therapists emerged to assist in the administration of oxygen therapy. Over time, the scope of practice expanded to include a wide range of therapeutic and diagnostic procedures.

In the 1950s and 1960s, the development of mechanical ventilation marked a significant milestone in respiratory care. This period also saw the establishment of formal education programs and professional organizations, such as the American Association for Respiratory Care (AARC), which played a crucial role in standardizing practices and promoting professional development.

Today, respiratory care is recognized as a specialized field requiring advanced education and training. Respiratory therapists are integral members of the healthcare team, working alongside physicians, nurses, and other healthcare professionals to provide comprehensive care to patients with respiratory conditions.

Core Principles of Respiratory Care

At the heart of respiratory care are several core principles that guide practice and ensure the delivery of high-quality care. These principles include:

- Patient-Centered Care: Respiratory therapists must prioritize the needs and preferences of patients, ensuring that care is tailored to individual circumstances and delivered with compassion and respect.
- Evidence-Based Practice: Effective respiratory care relies on the application of the best available evidence to clinical decision-making. This involves staying current with the latest research and incorporating evidence-based guidelines into practice.
- Interdisciplinary Collaboration: Respiratory care often requires collaboration with other healthcare professionals. Effective communication and teamwork are essential for coordinating care and achieving optimal patient outcomes.
- Continuous Improvement: Respiratory therapists should be committed to ongoing learning and quality improvement. This involves regularly assessing and enhancing their skills, knowledge, and practices to meet the evolving needs of patients.

Essential Skills for Respiratory Therapists

To deliver high-quality respiratory care, healthcare providers must possess a range of technical and interpersonal skills. Key competencies include:

- Clinical Assessment: The ability to perform thorough assessments of patients' respiratory status, including history taking, physical examination, and the interpretation of diagnostic tests.
- Therapeutic Interventions: Proficiency in administering a variety of respiratory therapies, such as oxygen therapy,

aerosol medication delivery, bronchial hygiene techniques, and mechanical ventilation.
- Patient Education: The capacity to educate patients and their families about respiratory conditions, treatment options, and self-management strategies.
- Critical Thinking: Strong problem-solving and decision-making skills are crucial for identifying and addressing complex respiratory issues.
- Communication: Effective verbal and written communication skills are essential for interacting with patients, families, and other healthcare team members.

The Respiratory Care Process

The respiratory care process is a systematic approach to patient management that includes assessment, diagnosis, planning, implementation, and evaluation. This process ensures that care is comprehensive, coordinated, and continuously refined to meet patients' needs.

- Assessment: Gathering comprehensive data about the patient's respiratory status, medical history, and current condition.
- Diagnosis: Identifying respiratory problems based on assessment findings and formulating a clinical diagnosis.
- Planning: Developing a care plan that outlines specific goals, interventions, and expected outcomes.
- Implementation: Executing the care plan by administering therapies, monitoring patient progress, and making necessary adjustments.
- Evaluation: Assessing the effectiveness of interventions and modifying the care plan as needed to achieve desired outcomes.

Understanding the fundamentals of respiratory care is essential for providing high-quality, safe, and effective treatment to patients with respiratory conditions.

DISCUSSION QUESTIONS

- How can understanding the basic principles of respiratory physiology and pathophysiology improve the quality and safety of respiratory care provided to patients?
- What are some common errors in respiratory care, and how can a strong foundation in respiratory fundamentals help in preventing these errors?

LESSON TWO: SAFETY PROTOCOLS IN RESPIRATORY CARE

Safety is a paramount concern in all areas of healthcare, and respiratory care is no exception. This lesson explores the critical safety protocols that respiratory therapists and healthcare providers must adhere to in order to protect patients, themselves, and their colleagues.

The Importance of Safety in Respiratory Care

Ensuring safety in respiratory care involves minimizing risks and preventing harm during the delivery of respiratory therapies and interventions. Respiratory therapists often work with vulnerable populations, including patients with chronic respiratory diseases, critically ill individuals, and those requiring mechanical ventilation. Therefore, strict adherence to safety protocols is essential to prevent adverse events and complications.

Infection Control

One of the most significant safety concerns in respiratory care is the prevention of infections. Respiratory therapists frequently handle equipment and perform procedures that can expose them and their patients to infectious agents. Key infection control practices include:

- Hand Hygiene: Consistent and thorough handwashing or the use of hand sanitizers before and after patient contact, and before handling respiratory equipment.

- Personal Protective Equipment (PPE): Proper use of gloves, masks, gowns, and eye protection to reduce the risk of transmitting infections.
- Sterilization and Disinfection: Ensuring that all respiratory equipment, such as ventilators, nebulizers, and oxygen delivery devices, are appropriately sterilized or disinfected between uses.
- Isolation Precautions: Implementing isolation protocols for patients with contagious respiratory infections to prevent the spread to others.

Medication Safety

Respiratory therapists often administer medications such as bronchodilators, corticosteroids, and antibiotics. Ensuring medication safety involves:

- Accurate Medication Administration: Verifying the correct medication, dose, route, and patient before administration.
- Monitoring for Adverse Reactions: Observing patients for potential side effects or adverse reactions to medications and responding promptly if they occur.
- Proper Storage and Handling: Storing medications correctly and handling them according to manufacturer guidelines to maintain their efficacy and safety.

Equipment Safety

The use of respiratory equipment, such as ventilators and oxygen therapy devices, requires careful attention to safety protocols:

- Regular Maintenance: Performing routine maintenance and checks on equipment to ensure it is functioning correctly and safely.
- Proper Setup and Use: Following manufacturer instructions and clinical guidelines for setting up and using respiratory equipment to prevent malfunctions and misuse.

- Training and Competency: Ensuring that all respiratory therapists and healthcare providers are adequately trained and competent in the use of respiratory equipment.

Patient Safety

Patient safety is at the heart of all respiratory care practices. Key strategies for ensuring patient safety include:

- Patient Identification: Verifying the identity of patients before providing any treatment or procedure to prevent errors.
- Fall Prevention: Implementing measures to prevent falls, particularly for patients who may be weak or disoriented due to their respiratory condition.
- Monitoring and Alarms: Using monitoring devices and alarms to continuously assess patients' respiratory status and promptly address any changes or emergencies.
- Documentation and Communication: Maintaining accurate and up-to-date documentation of patient care and effectively communicating with other healthcare team members to ensure continuity and coordination of care.

Emergency Preparedness

Being prepared for emergencies is a critical aspect of respiratory care safety. This includes:

- Emergency Protocols: Familiarizing oneself with and adhering to emergency protocols for situations such as respiratory distress, cardiac arrest, or equipment failure.
- Simulation Training: Participating in simulation training exercises to practice and refine emergency response skills.
- Availability of Emergency Equipment: Ensuring that emergency equipment, such as resuscitation bags, suction devices, and defibrillators, are readily available and in good working condition.

Safety protocols are fundamental to the practice of respiratory care, ensuring that both patients and healthcare providers are protected from harm. By adhering to stringent infection control measures, medication safety practices, equipment maintenance, patient safety strategies, and emergency preparedness protocols, respiratory therapists can deliver high-quality care while minimizing risks.

DISCUSSION QUESTIONS

- What are the critical components of effective safety protocols in respiratory care, and how can healthcare providers ensure consistent implementation and adherence to these protocols?
- How can respiratory care teams be trained and motivated to prioritize safety protocols in their daily practice, and what role does leadership play in fostering a culture of safety?

MODULE TWO

LESSON ONE: QUALITY IMPROVEMENT IN RESPIRATORY CARE

Quality improvement (QI) is a systematic approach to enhancing the standard of care provided to patients. In respiratory care, QI initiatives aim to improve patient outcomes, increase efficiency, and ensure that care is patient-centered. This lesson delves into the principles and methods of quality improvement in respiratory care and provides practical guidance for implementing QI initiatives.

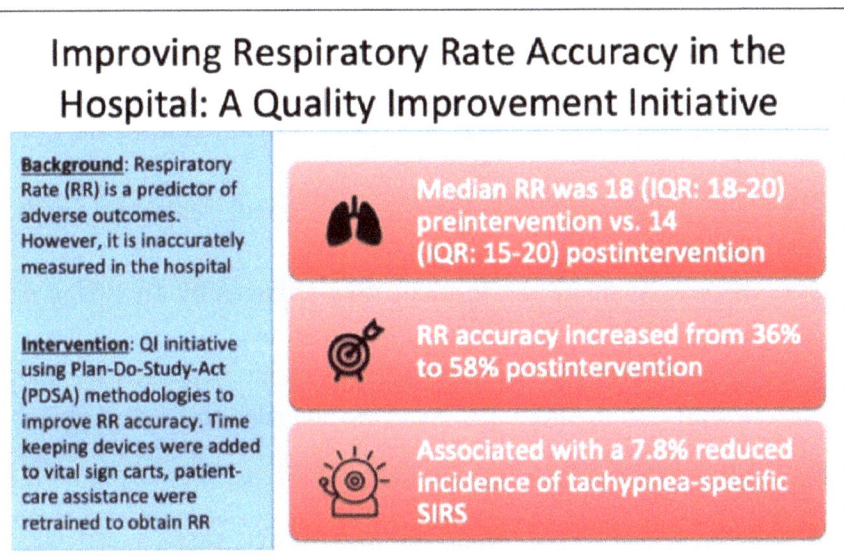

Understanding Quality Improvement

Quality improvement involves the continuous assessment and refinement of healthcare processes to achieve better patient outcomes and greater efficiency. It is an ongoing effort that requires the collaboration of all members of the healthcare team. Key principles of QI include:

- Patient-Centeredness: Placing the needs and preferences of patients at the forefront of improvement efforts.
- Data-Driven Decision Making: Using data to identify areas for improvement, set goals, and measure the impact of changes.
- Interdisciplinary Collaboration: Engaging all members of the healthcare team in QI initiatives to leverage diverse perspectives and expertise.
- Continuous Learning: Committing to ongoing education and adaptation to incorporate new evidence and best practices into care.

The Quality Improvement Process

The QI process typically follows a structured framework, such as the Plan-Do-Study-Act (PDSA) cycle:

- Plan: Identify an area for improvement, gather data, and develop a plan for making changes.
- Do: Implement the changes on a small scale to test their impact.
- Study: Evaluate the results of the changes by analyzing data and comparing outcomes to the baseline.
- Act: Based on the evaluation, decide whether to adopt, modify, or abandon the changes, and plan the next steps.

Identifying Areas for Improvement

In respiratory care, QI initiatives can target various aspects of practice, including:

- Clinical Outcomes: Improving patient outcomes such as reduced hospital readmissions, decreased incidence of ventilator-associated pneumonia (VAP), and better management of chronic respiratory diseases.
- Process Efficiency: Streamlining processes to reduce delays, eliminate waste, and enhance the overall efficiency of care delivery.

- Patient Experience: Enhancing patient satisfaction by improving communication, reducing wait times, and ensuring that care is respectful and responsive to patient needs.
- Safety: Reducing the risk of errors and adverse events through rigorous safety protocols and continuous monitoring.

Implementing Quality Improvement Initiatives

Successful QI initiatives require careful planning and execution. Steps to implement QI initiatives in respiratory care include:

- Forming a QI Team: Assemble a team of healthcare professionals with diverse skills and perspectives to lead the QI efforts.
- Setting Goals: Define clear, measurable goals for the improvement initiative.
- Collecting Data: Gather baseline data to understand the current state and identify specific areas for improvement.
- Developing Interventions: Design interventions aimed at achieving the set goals. This may involve changes to clinical practices, workflows, or patient education strategies.
- Testing and Evaluating: Implement the interventions on a small scale, collect data, and evaluate their impact. Use the PDSA cycle to refine the interventions based on the evaluation.
- Scaling Up: If the interventions are successful, implement them on a larger scale and continue to monitor their impact.

Case Study: Reducing Ventilator-Associated Pneumonia

- Ventilator-associated pneumonia (VAP) is a significant concern in respiratory care. A successful QI initiative to reduce VAP might involve the following steps:
- Identifying the Problem: High rates of VAP in the intensive care unit (ICU) are impacting patient outcomes.
- Setting a Goal: Reduce the incidence of VAP by 50% within six months.

- Collecting Data: Gather baseline data on VAP rates and identify contributing factors.
- Developing Interventions: Implement evidence-based practices such as elevating the head of the bed, using subglottic suctioning, and ensuring hand hygiene compliance.
- Testing and Evaluating: Conduct a pilot study in one ICU unit, monitor VAP rates, and gather feedback from staff.
- Scaling Up: If the pilot is successful, roll out the interventions across all ICU units and continue to monitor VAP rates.

Sustaining Quality Improvement

Sustaining the gains achieved through QI initiatives requires ongoing commitment and vigilance. Strategies for sustaining QI include:

- Embedding QI in Organizational Culture: Foster a culture of continuous improvement where all staff are encouraged to contribute to QI efforts.
- Regular Monitoring: Continuously collect and analyze data to ensure that improvements are maintained and to identify new areas for improvement.
- Ongoing Education: Provide regular training and education to keep staff informed about best practices and new evidence.
- Celebrating Success: Recognize and celebrate the achievements of QI initiatives to motivate and engage staff.

Quality improvement is a vital aspect of respiratory care, driving better patient outcomes, greater efficiency, and enhanced patient experiences. By understanding the principles and processes of QI, identifying areas for improvement, implementing effective interventions, and sustaining the gains, respiratory therapists can make a significant impact on the quality of care they provide.

DISCUSSION QUESTIONS

- What strategies can be employed to identify areas for quality improvement in respiratory care, and how can healthcare providers effectively implement these improvements to enhance patient outcomes?
- How can the use of evidence-based practices and guidelines contribute to the continuous quality improvement process in respiratory care?

LESSON TWO: PATIENT ASSESSMENT AND MONITORING

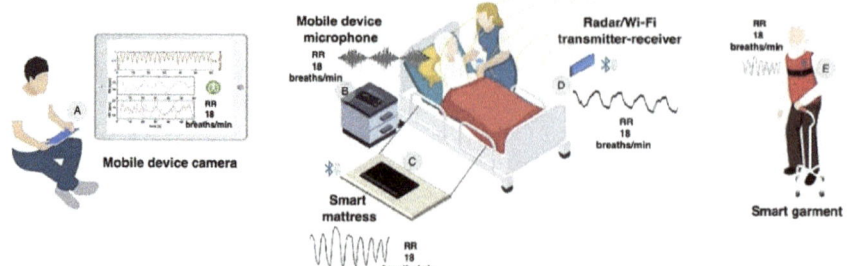

Effective patient assessment and monitoring are critical components of respiratory care. These processes enable healthcare providers to evaluate respiratory function, diagnose conditions, and monitor the progress of treatment. This lesson delves into the methods and tools used for assessing and monitoring patients with respiratory conditions, emphasizing the importance of thorough and accurate evaluation.

The Importance of Patient Assessment

Patient assessment is the foundation of respiratory care. A comprehensive assessment allows healthcare providers to:

- Identify Respiratory Problems: Detect and diagnose respiratory conditions such as asthma, chronic obstructive pulmonary disease (COPD), pneumonia, and respiratory failure.
- Develop Treatment Plans: Create individualized treatment plans based on the specific needs and conditions of patients.
- Monitor Progress: Track the effectiveness of treatments and make necessary adjustments to optimize patient outcomes.
- Prevent Complications: Identify early signs of complications and intervene promptly to prevent worsening of the condition.

Components of a Comprehensive Respiratory Assessment

A thorough respiratory assessment involves several key components:

- Patient History: Collecting a detailed medical history, including information about respiratory symptoms, past medical conditions, family history, and lifestyle factors such as smoking.
- Physical Examination: Performing a physical examination to assess respiratory function, including inspection, palpation, percussion, and auscultation of the chest.
- Diagnostic Tests: Utilizing various diagnostic tests and tools to evaluate respiratory function and diagnose conditions.

Patient History

The patient history provides valuable information that can guide the assessment and diagnosis. Key elements to inquire about include:

- Chief Complaint: Understanding the primary reason for the patient's visit, such as shortness of breath, cough, or wheezing.
- History of Present Illness: Gathering detailed information about the onset, duration, and characteristics of respiratory symptoms.
- Past Medical History: Reviewing past medical conditions, surgeries, hospitalizations, and treatments related to respiratory health.
- Family History: Identifying any family history of respiratory diseases or conditions.
- Social History: Considering lifestyle factors such as smoking, occupational exposures, and environmental influences that may impact respiratory health.

Physical Examination

The physical examination involves several techniques to assess respiratory function:

- Inspection: Observing the patient's overall appearance, respiratory rate and pattern, use of accessory muscles, and any signs of respiratory distress.
- Palpation: Feeling the chest wall to assess for tenderness, symmetry, and tactile fremitus (vibrations transmitted through the chest wall).
- Percussion: Tapping on the chest to evaluate the underlying structures and detect areas of abnormality such as consolidation or hyperinflation.
- Auscultation: Listening to breath sounds using a stethoscope to identify normal and abnormal sounds such as wheezes, crackles, and diminished breath sounds.

Diagnostic Tests and Tools

Several diagnostic tests and tools are used in respiratory care to assess and monitor patients:

- Pulmonary Function Tests (PFTs): Measure lung volumes, capacities, and flow rates to evaluate respiratory function and diagnose conditions such as asthma and COPD.
- Arterial Blood Gas (ABG) Analysis: Assesses oxygenation, ventilation, and acid-base status by analyzing a sample of arterial blood.
- Chest X-ray: Provides imaging of the chest to identify abnormalities such as infections, tumors, and structural changes.
- Computed Tomography (CT) Scan: Offers detailed cross-sectional imaging of the chest to detect and evaluate respiratory conditions.
- Pulse Oximetry: Measures oxygen saturation levels in the blood using a non-invasive sensor placed on the fingertip.
- Capnography: Monitors the concentration of carbon dioxide in exhaled air to assess ventilation and detect respiratory compromise.

Monitoring Respiratory Function

Continuous monitoring of respiratory function is essential for managing patients with respiratory conditions. Key aspects of monitoring include:

- Vital Signs: Regularly measuring and recording vital signs such as respiratory rate, heart rate, blood pressure, and oxygen saturation.
- Breath Sounds: Periodically auscultating breath sounds to detect changes and monitor the effectiveness of treatments.
- Spirometry: Conducting periodic spirometry tests to assess lung function and track the progress of conditions such as asthma and COPD.
- Patient Self-Monitoring: Educating patients on how to monitor their own respiratory symptoms and use tools such as peak flow meters at home.

Case Study: Managing Asthma in a Pediatric Patient

A comprehensive assessment and monitoring plan for a pediatric patient with asthma might include the following steps:

- Patient History: Gathering detailed information about the child's asthma symptoms, triggers, and past treatments.
- Physical Examination: Conducting a thorough examination, focusing on breath sounds, respiratory rate, and signs of distress.
- Pulmonary Function Tests: Performing spirometry to assess lung function and determine the severity of asthma.
- Monitoring Plan: Establishing a monitoring plan that includes regular follow-up visits, spirometry tests, and the use of a peak flow meter at home.
- Patient Education: Educating the child and their family about asthma management, including the use of inhalers, avoidance of triggers, and action plans for exacerbations.

Patient assessment and monitoring are fundamental to the practice of respiratory care. By conducting comprehensive assessments, utilizing appropriate diagnostic tools, and implementing effective monitoring strategies, healthcare providers can ensure that patients with respiratory conditions receive the highest quality of care.

DISCUSSION QUESTIONS

- How can healthcare providers ensure that their respiratory assessments are thorough and comprehensive, and what specific techniques or tools can be utilized to enhance the accuracy of these assessments?
- What are the key indicators and signs that healthcare providers should prioritize during patient assessments to effectively identify respiratory conditions early and accurately?

MODULE THREE

LESSON ONE: TECHNOLOGICAL ADVANCES IN RESPIRATORY CARE

Technological advancements have revolutionized the field of respiratory care, providing healthcare providers with new tools and techniques to improve patient outcomes. This lesson explores the latest technological innovations in respiratory care, including their applications, benefits, and challenges.

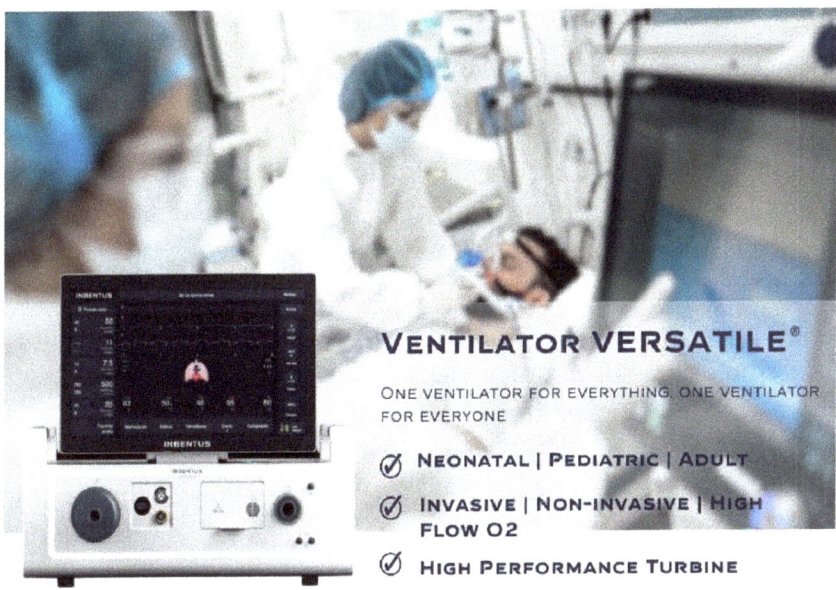

The Impact of Technology on Respiratory Care

Technology has significantly enhanced the ability to diagnose, treat, and manage respiratory conditions. Key areas where technology has made a substantial impact include:

- Diagnostic Tools: Advanced imaging and testing technologies provide more accurate and detailed information about respiratory conditions.
- Therapeutic Devices: Innovations in therapeutic devices have improved the effectiveness and comfort of respiratory treatments.
- Monitoring Systems: Sophisticated monitoring systems enable continuous and real-time assessment of patients' respiratory status.
- Telemedicine: Telemedicine technologies facilitate remote consultations and monitoring, increasing access to respiratory care.

Advanced Diagnostic Tools

Advanced diagnostic tools have improved the accuracy and speed of diagnosing respiratory conditions:

- High-Resolution Computed Tomography (HRCT): Provides detailed imaging of the lungs, allowing for the detection of subtle abnormalities that may not be visible on standard chest X-rays.
- Bronchoscopy: A minimally invasive procedure that allows direct visualization of the airways and collection of tissue samples for diagnosis.
- Biomarker Testing: The use of biomarkers to identify specific respiratory conditions, such as eosinophilic inflammation in asthma, which can guide targeted therapies.

Innovative Therapeutic Devices

Recent advancements in therapeutic devices have enhanced the delivery and effectiveness of respiratory treatments:

- Smart Inhalers: Equipped with sensors that track medication use and provide feedback to patients and healthcare providers, improving adherence and management of conditions like asthma.

- Non-Invasive Ventilation (NIV): Devices that provide ventilatory support without the need for intubation, offering a less invasive option for patients with respiratory failure.
- High-Flow Nasal Cannula (HFNC): Delivers heated and humidified oxygen at high flow rates, improving patient comfort and oxygenation.

Advanced Monitoring Systems

Modern monitoring systems enable continuous and precise assessment of respiratory function:

- Remote Monitoring Devices: Wearable devices and home monitoring systems that allow for continuous tracking of respiratory parameters such as oxygen saturation, respiratory rate, and peak flow.
- Capnography: Advanced capnography systems provide real-time monitoring of end-tidal CO_2, helping to assess ventilation status and detect respiratory compromise.
- Artificial Intelligence (AI) and Machine Learning: AI algorithms analyze data from monitoring systems to identify patterns, predict exacerbations, and guide clinical decision-making.

Telemedicine in Respiratory Care

Telemedicine has become increasingly important in respiratory care, particularly in the context of the COVID-19 pandemic:

- Remote Consultations: Virtual visits enable patients to receive care from respiratory specialists without the need for travel, increasing access to care.
- Telemonitoring: Remote monitoring of patients with chronic respiratory conditions, such as COPD and asthma, allows for early detection of exacerbations and timely interventions.
- Tele-rehabilitation: Virtual pulmonary rehabilitation programs provide patients with exercises, education, and support remotely, improving their quality of life and reducing hospital admissions.

Challenges and Considerations

While technological advancements offer numerous benefits, they also present challenges and considerations:

- Cost and Accessibility: Advanced technologies can be expensive, and access may be limited in low-resource settings.
- Training and Competency: Healthcare providers must receive proper training to effectively use new technologies and integrate them into practice.
- Data Privacy and Security: The use of digital tools and remote monitoring systems raises concerns about the privacy and security of patient data.
- Patient Acceptance and Adherence: Patients may be hesitant to adopt new technologies or may struggle with using them correctly, impacting their effectiveness.

Case Study: Implementing Telemedicine for COPD Management

A case study of implementing telemedicine for managing patients with COPD might include the following steps:

- Identifying the Need: Recognizing that patients with COPD in rural areas have limited access to respiratory specialists.
- Selecting Technology: Choosing a telemedicine platform that includes remote monitoring devices for tracking respiratory parameters.
- Training Healthcare Providers: Providing training for healthcare providers on how to conduct virtual consultations and interpret data from remote monitoring devices.
- Patient Education: Educating patients on how to use the telemedicine platform and remote monitoring devices, and addressing any concerns or barriers.
- Evaluating Outcomes: Monitoring the impact of telemedicine on patient outcomes, such as hospital readmissions, exacerbation rates, and patient satisfaction.

Technological advancements have transformed respiratory care, offering new tools and techniques that enhance diagnosis, treatment, and monitoring. By embracing these innovations, healthcare providers can improve patient outcomes and deliver more efficient and effective care. However, it is essential to address the challenges and considerations associated with these technologies to ensure their successful implementation and integration into practice.

DISCUSSION QUESTIONS

- How have recent technological advances, such as telemedicine and remote monitoring, improved the management of chronic respiratory conditions and patient outcomes?
- In what ways can artificial intelligence and machine learning be utilized to enhance diagnostic accuracy and personalize treatment plans in respiratory care?

LESSON TWO: EMERGENCY MANAGEMENT IN RESPIRATORY CARE

Emergencies in respiratory care require swift and effective responses to prevent life-threatening complications. This lesson explores the key principles and practices of emergency management in respiratory care, including the identification and management of common respiratory emergencies, the use of emergency equipment, and the importance of teamwork and communication.

Management of Respiratory Emergencies

Basic Principles
- Maintain the airway.
  - Protect the cervical spine if trauma is suspected.
- Patients breathing inadequately should be assisted with artificial ventilation.
- Any patient with respiratory distress should receive oxygen.
- Oxygen should never be withheld from a patient suspected of suffering from hypoxia.

Principles of Emergency Management

Effective emergency management in respiratory care involves several key principles:

- Rapid Assessment: Quickly assessing the patient's condition to identify the nature and severity of the emergency.
- Prioritization: Prioritizing interventions based on the patient's needs and the urgency of the situation.
- Preparedness: Ensuring that all healthcare providers are prepared and trained to handle respiratory emergencies.

- Communication: Maintaining clear and effective communication among the healthcare team to coordinate care and ensure timely interventions.

Common Respiratory Emergencies

Respiratory emergencies can arise from various conditions and require prompt recognition and management:

- Acute Respiratory Distress Syndrome (ARDS): A severe condition characterized by rapid onset of widespread inflammation in the lungs, leading to respiratory failure.
- Asthma Exacerbation: A sudden worsening of asthma symptoms that can lead to respiratory distress and failure if not promptly treated.
- Chronic Obstructive Pulmonary Disease (COPD) Exacerbation: An acute worsening of COPD symptoms, often triggered by infections or environmental factors.
- Pulmonary Embolism: A blockage in one of the pulmonary arteries, usually caused by a blood clot, leading to impaired oxygenation and respiratory distress.
- Pneumothorax: The presence of air in the pleural space, causing lung collapse and respiratory distress.
- Foreign Body Aspiration: Inhalation of an object that obstructs the airway, leading to choking and respiratory distress.

Emergency Equipment

Having the right emergency equipment readily available and in good working condition is crucial for managing respiratory emergencies:

- Bag-Valve-Mask (BVM) Resuscitators: Used to provide positive pressure ventilation to patients who are not breathing adequately.
- Oxygen Delivery Devices: Including nasal cannulas, face masks, and non-rebreather masks to provide supplemental oxygen.

- Airway Management Tools: Such as oropharyngeal and nasopharyngeal airways, laryngoscopes, endotracheal tubes, and suction devices.
- Mechanical Ventilators: For providing advanced ventilatory support to patients in respiratory failure.
- Emergency Medications: Including bronchodilators, corticosteroids, and epinephrine for managing asthma exacerbations, allergic reactions, and other emergencies.

Teamwork and Communication

Effective management of respiratory emergencies requires teamwork and clear communication among healthcare providers:

- Roles and Responsibilities: Clearly defining roles and responsibilities for each team member during an emergency to ensure coordinated and efficient care.
- Communication Protocols: Establishing communication protocols to relay critical information quickly and accurately.
- Simulation Training: Conducting regular simulation training exercises to practice emergency scenarios and improve team coordination and response.

Case Study: Managing an Asthma Exacerbation

A case study of managing a severe asthma exacerbation might include the following steps:

- Rapid Assessment: Quickly assessing the patient's respiratory status, including breath sounds, respiratory rate, and oxygen saturation.
- Administering Medications: Providing fast-acting bronchodilators, such as albuterol, and corticosteroids to reduce inflammation.
- Oxygen Therapy: Administering supplemental oxygen to maintain adequate oxygenation.
- Monitoring: Continuously monitoring the patient's respiratory status and vital signs.

- Escalation of Care: If the patient's condition does not improve, escalating care to include non-invasive ventilation or intubation and mechanical ventilation.

Emergency management is a critical aspect of respiratory care, requiring rapid assessment, prioritization, preparedness, and effective communication. By understanding the principles of emergency management, recognizing common respiratory emergencies, ensuring the availability of emergency equipment, and fostering teamwork and communication, healthcare providers can deliver prompt and effective care during respiratory emergencies.

DISCUSSION QUESTIONS

- What are the essential components of an effective emergency management plan for respiratory care, and how can healthcare providers ensure they are adequately prepared to handle respiratory emergencies?
- How can simulation training and regular drills improve the readiness and response of respiratory care teams during emergency situations?

MODULE FOUR

LESSON ONE: CHRONIC RESPIRATORY DISEASE MANAGEMENT

Managing chronic respiratory diseases requires a comprehensive and patient-centered approach. This lesson explores the key strategies for managing common chronic respiratory diseases, including asthma, chronic obstructive pulmonary disease (COPD), and interstitial lung disease (ILD). It also highlights the importance of patient education, lifestyle modifications, and multidisciplinary care.

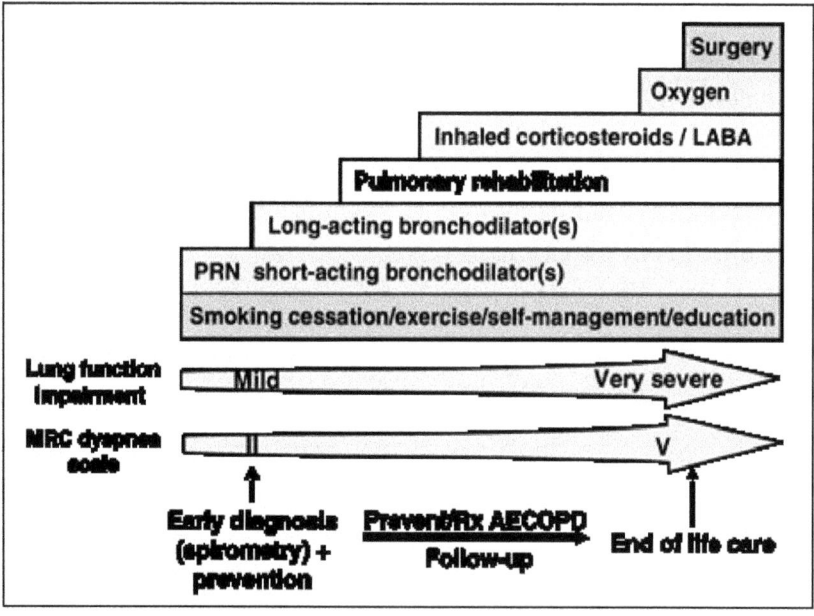

Asthma Management

Asthma is a chronic inflammatory disease of the airways characterized by recurrent episodes of wheezing, shortness of breath, chest tightness, and coughing. Effective management involves:

- Patient Education: Teaching patients about asthma, its triggers, and how to manage symptoms and prevent exacerbations.
- Medication Management: Using a stepwise approach to pharmacotherapy, including the use of inhaled corticosteroids, long-acting beta-agonists, and leukotriene modifiers.
- Trigger Avoidance: Identifying and avoiding environmental and occupational triggers that can exacerbate asthma symptoms.
- Action Plans: Developing individualized asthma action plans that outline steps to take during an exacerbation.

Chronic Obstructive Pulmonary Disease (COPD) Management

COPD is a progressive disease characterized by airflow limitation and chronic respiratory symptoms. Management strategies include:

- Smoking Cessation: Encouraging and supporting patients to quit smoking, the most important intervention for slowing disease progression.
- Pharmacotherapy: Using bronchodilators, inhaled corticosteroids, and phosphodiesterase-4 inhibitors to manage symptoms and prevent exacerbations.
- Pulmonary Rehabilitation: Implementing comprehensive pulmonary rehabilitation programs that include exercise training, education, and psychosocial support.
- Oxygen Therapy: Providing long-term oxygen therapy for patients with chronic hypoxemia to improve survival and quality of life.

Interstitial Lung Disease (ILD) Management

ILD encompasses a group of disorders characterized by inflammation and fibrosis of the lung tissue. Management approaches include:

- Accurate Diagnosis: Conducting thorough assessments and utilizing high-resolution computed tomography (HRCT) and lung biopsies to accurately diagnose ILD subtypes.

- Anti-Inflammatory and Antifibrotic Therapy: Using medications such as corticosteroids, immunosuppressants, and antifibrotic agents to manage inflammation and fibrosis.
- Supportive Care: Providing supportive care, including oxygen therapy, pulmonary rehabilitation, and symptom management.
- Patient Education and Counseling: Educating patients about their condition, treatment options, and the importance of adhering to treatment plans.

Multidisciplinary Care

Managing chronic respiratory diseases often requires a multidisciplinary approach involving various healthcare professionals:

- Respiratory Therapists: Providing respiratory therapies, education, and support to patients.
- Pulmonologists: Diagnosing and managing complex respiratory conditions.
- Primary Care Providers: Coordinating overall care and managing comorbidities.
- Nurses: Offering patient education, support, and monitoring.
- Pharmacists: Assisting with medication management and adherence.
- Dietitians: Providing nutritional support and counseling.
- Psychologists: Addressing the psychological and emotional aspects of living with a chronic respiratory disease.

Lifestyle Modifications

Encouraging patients to make lifestyle modifications can significantly impact the management of chronic respiratory diseases:

- Healthy Diet: Promoting a balanced diet rich in fruits, vegetables, and whole grains to support overall health.

- Regular Exercise: Encouraging regular physical activity to improve cardiovascular fitness, muscle strength, and overall well-being.
- Weight Management: Supporting patients in achieving and maintaining a healthy weight to reduce the burden on the respiratory system.
- Stress Management: Teaching techniques for managing stress, which can exacerbate respiratory symptoms.

Effective management of chronic respiratory diseases requires a comprehensive and patient-centered approach, including patient education, medication management, lifestyle modifications, and multidisciplinary care.

DISCUSSION QUESTIONS

- How can healthcare providers effectively educate patients with chronic respiratory diseases on self-management techniques, and what impact does this education have on disease control and patient quality of life?
- What role do support groups and community resources play in the management of chronic respiratory diseases, and how can patients be encouraged to utilize these resources?

MODULE FIVE

LESSON TWO: RESPIRATORY CARE IN SPECIAL POPULATIONS

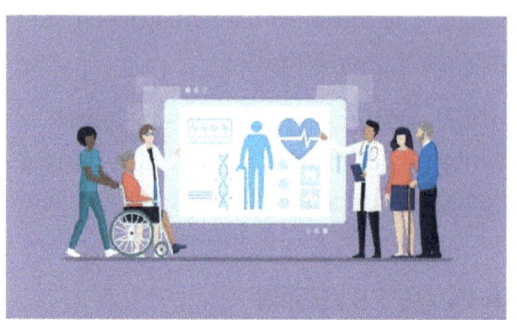

Providing respiratory care to special populations requires an understanding of their unique needs and considerations. This lesson explores respiratory care for neonates, pediatric patients, geriatric patients, and patients with neuromuscular diseases, highlighting the specific challenges and approaches for each population.

NEONATAL RESPIRATORY CARE

Neonates, especially preterm infants, are at high risk for respiratory complications. Key aspects of neonatal respiratory care include:

Respiratory Distress Syndrome (RDS):

- Management: RDS is treated with surfactant therapy to reduce surface tension in the lungs and mechanical ventilation to support breathing.
- Prevention: Administering antenatal steroids to mothers at risk of preterm delivery to accelerate fetal lung maturation.

Bronchopulmonary Dysplasia (BPD):

- Long-term Support: Providing ongoing respiratory support, monitoring, and management for infants who develop BPD as a result of prolonged mechanical ventilation or oxygen therapy.
- Nutritional Support: Ensuring adequate nutrition to support lung growth and repair.

Non-Invasive Ventilation:

- CPAP: Continuous Positive Airway Pressure (CPAP) is used to maintain airway patency and reduce the need for intubation and mechanical ventilation.
- Nasal Cannulas: High-flow nasal cannula (HFNC) therapy can also provide respiratory support with less discomfort for the neonate.

Family-Centered Care:

- Parental Involvement: Involving parents in the care process, providing education about their infant's condition and care needs, and offering emotional support.
- Skin-to-Skin Contact: Encouraging practices such as kangaroo care to promote bonding and support the infant's respiratory stability.

PEDIATRIC RESPIRATORY CARE

Pediatric patients, ranging from infants to adolescents, require age-appropriate respiratory care:

Asthma Management:

- Education: Teaching children and their families about asthma triggers, medication use, and action plans for exacerbations.
- Environmental Control: Identifying and minimizing exposure to asthma triggers in the child's environment.

Cystic Fibrosis (CF):

- Multidisciplinary Approach: Involving a team of specialists, including pulmonologists, nutritionists, and physical therapists, to manage the complex needs of children with CF.
- Airway Clearance Techniques: Using chest physiotherapy, oscillating positive expiratory pressure (OPEP) devices, and inhaled medications to maintain airway patency and reduce infections.

Acute Respiratory Infections:

- Prompt Treatment: Providing timely treatment for respiratory infections, such as pneumonia or bronchiolitis, to prevent complications.
- Vaccination: Ensuring up-to-date vaccinations to prevent common respiratory infections like influenza and pertussis.

Congenital Conditions:

- Tracheostomy Care: For children with tracheostomies, providing specialized care, including cleaning, suctioning, and monitoring for complications.
- Ongoing Monitoring: Regular follow-up and monitoring for conditions like congenital diaphragmatic hernia or tracheomalacia.

GERIATRIC RESPIRATORY CARE

Elderly patients often have multiple comorbidities that impact respiratory health. Key aspects of geriatric respiratory care include:

Chronic Disease Management:

- COPD: Managing chronic obstructive pulmonary disease with bronchodilators, corticosteroids, and pulmonary rehabilitation.
- Heart Failure: Addressing the interplay between heart failure and respiratory function to optimize overall health.

Frailty and Mobility:

- Physical Therapy: Implementing pulmonary rehabilitation and physical therapy to improve respiratory muscle strength and overall mobility.
- Fall Prevention: Ensuring safety measures to prevent falls, which can lead to further respiratory complications.

Polypharmacy:

- Medication Review: Regularly reviewing medications to avoid drug interactions and ensure that respiratory treatments are effective and safe.
- Simplified Regimens: Simplifying medication regimens to enhance adherence and reduce confusion.

Palliative Care:

- Symptom Management: Providing palliative care to manage symptoms such as dyspnea and anxiety in patients with advanced respiratory diseases.
- Advance Care Planning: Discussing and documenting patients' preferences for end-of-life care.

RESPIRATORY CARE FOR PATIENTS WITH NEUROMUSCULAR DISEASES

Patients with neuromuscular diseases, such as amyotrophic lateral sclerosis (ALS) or muscular dystrophy, require specialized respiratory care:

Ventilatory Support:

- Non-Invasive Ventilation (NIV): Using NIV to support breathing, particularly during sleep, to reduce the risk of respiratory failure.
- Mechanical Ventilation: In advanced stages, invasive mechanical ventilation may be necessary to support respiration.

Airway Clearance:

- Assisted Coughing: Utilizing techniques and devices to assist with coughing and clearing secretions.
- Suctioning: Regular suctioning to maintain airway patency and prevent infections.

Nutritional Support:

- Swallowing Assessment: Regular assessment of swallowing function to prevent aspiration and provide appropriate nutritional support.
- Enteral Feeding: Implementing enteral feeding if oral intake becomes unsafe or insufficient.

Multidisciplinary Care:

- Team Approach: Involving a multidisciplinary team, including neurologists, respiratory therapists, speech therapists, and dietitians, to provide comprehensive care.
- Patient and Family Education: Educating patients and their families about disease progression, respiratory care techniques, and equipment use.

DISCUSSION QUESTIONS

- How can respiratory care be tailored to meet the specific needs of neonates and pediatric patients, and what unique challenges do healthcare providers face when caring for these populations?
- What considerations must be taken into account when providing respiratory care to geriatric patients, particularly those with multiple comorbidities and age-related physiological changes?

MODULE SIX

LESSON ONE: ETHICAL AND LEGAL CONSIDERATIONS IN RESPIRATORY CARE

Ethical and legal considerations are integral to the practice of respiratory care. This lesson explores the key ethical principles and legal issues that respiratory therapists and healthcare providers must navigate, including patient autonomy, confidentiality, informed consent, and professional conduct.

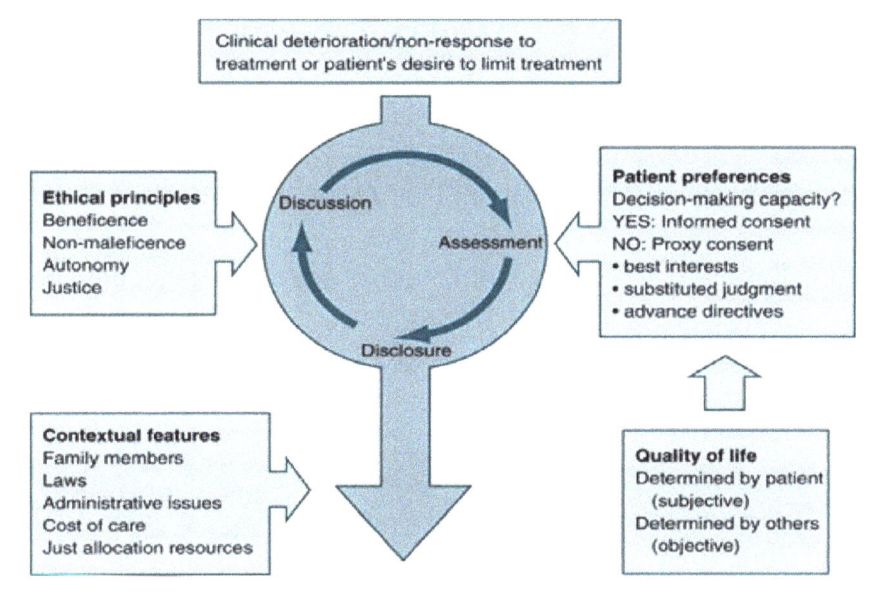

Clinical deterioration/non-response to treatment or patient's desire to limit treatment

Ethical principles
- Beneficence
- Non-maleficence
- Autonomy
- Justice

Discussion → Assessment → Disclosure

Patient preferences
- Decision-making capacity?
- YES: Informed consent
- NO: Proxy consent
  - best interests
  - substituted judgment
  - advance directives

Contextual features
- Family members
- Laws
- Administrative issues
- Cost of care
- Just allocation resources

Quality of life
- Determined by patient (subjective)
- Determined by others (objective)

ETHICAL PRINCIPLES IN RESPIRATORY CARE

Autonomy:

- Respecting Patient Decisions: Respecting patients' rights to make informed decisions about their own care, including the right to accept or refuse treatment.
- Advance Directives: Encouraging patients to complete advance directives to guide care decisions in situations where they may be unable to communicate their wishes.

Beneficence:
- Acting in the Patient's Best Interest: Providing care that benefits the patient and promotes their well-being.
- Balancing Risks and Benefits: Carefully considering the risks and benefits of treatment options to ensure that interventions provide the greatest overall benefit to the patient.

Non-Maleficence:
- Do No Harm: Avoiding actions that could cause harm to the patient, whether through action or inaction.
- Risk Management: Implementing strategies to minimize potential harm, such as adhering to evidence-based practices and guidelines.

Justice:
- Fairness in Care: Ensuring that all patients receive equitable access to respiratory care services.
- Resource Allocation: Making fair decisions regarding the allocation of limited resources, such as ventilators during a pandemic.

Confidentiality:
- Protecting Patient Information: Safeguarding patients' personal health information and sharing it only with authorized individuals.
- HIPAA Compliance: Adhering to the Health Insurance Portability and Accountability Act (HIPAA) regulations to protect patient privacy.

LEGAL CONSIDERATIONS IN RESPIRATORY CARE

Informed Consent:
- Patient Education: Ensuring that patients are fully informed about the nature of their condition, proposed treatments, potential risks, benefits, and alternatives.

- Voluntary Decision-Making: Confirming that patients give their consent voluntarily, without coercion or undue influence.

Scope of Practice:

- Professional Boundaries: Understanding and adhering to the defined scope of practice for respiratory therapists and other healthcare providers.
- State Regulations: Complying with state-specific regulations and licensure requirements that govern respiratory care practice.

Documentation:

- Accurate Record-Keeping: Maintaining accurate and comprehensive medical records to support patient care and protect against legal issues.
- Legal Documentation: Ensuring that all documentation meets legal standards and accurately reflects the care provided.

Professional Liability:

- Malpractice: Understanding the legal implications of malpractice and the importance of providing care that meets accepted standards of practice.
- Risk Mitigation: Implementing practices to reduce the risk of legal action, such as continuous education, adherence to guidelines, and effective communication with patients and their families.

End-of-Life Care:

- Ethical Decision-Making: Navigating the ethical complexities of end-of-life care, including decisions about withholding or withdrawing life-sustaining treatments.
- Legal Directives: Respecting and implementing legal directives such as Do Not Resuscitate (DNR) orders and living wills.

CASE STUDY: NAVIGATING ETHICAL AND LEGAL ISSUES IN END-OF-LIFE CARE

A case study exploring the ethical and legal considerations in end-of-life care for a patient with advanced chronic obstructive pulmonary disease (COPD):

- Patient Background: The patient, a 75-year-old male with advanced COPD, has a history of multiple hospitalizations for exacerbations. He has expressed a desire to avoid prolonged life support and has a living will that includes a DNR order.
- Ethical Considerations: The healthcare team must balance the patient's autonomy and expressed wishes with the principles of beneficence and non-maleficence. They must also consider the emotional and ethical impact on the patient's family.
- Legal Considerations: The team must ensure that all care decisions comply with the patient's legal directives and state regulations regarding end-of-life care.
- Team Discussion: The healthcare team, including the pulmonologist, respiratory therapist, nurse, and social worker, convenes to discuss the patient's condition and care plan. They review the patient's living will and ensure that all team members understand and respect the patient's wishes.
- Patient and Family Communication: The team meets with the patient and his family to discuss the care plan, reaffirm the patient's wishes, and provide support. They explain the implications of the DNR order and ensure that the family is fully informed and involved in the decision-making process.
- Implementation: The team implements a care plan that focuses on comfort and palliative care, respecting the patient's wishes and legal directives. They provide ongoing support to the patient and his family throughout the end-of-life process.

Ethical and legal considerations are fundamental to the practice of respiratory care. By understanding and applying the principles of autonomy, beneficence, non-maleficence, justice, and confidentiality, healthcare providers can navigate complex situations and provide compassionate, patient-centered care. Legal considerations, including informed consent, scope of practice, documentation, professional liability, and end-of-life care, are essential to ensuring that care is provided within the framework of regulatory and legal requirements.

DISCUSSION QUESTIONS

- How can healthcare providers navigate the ethical challenges of balancing patient autonomy with beneficence and non-maleficence in respiratory care decisions?
- What strategies can be employed to ensure that advance directives and patient preferences are respected and integrated into the care plan, particularly in end-of-life scenarios?

MODULE SEVEN

LESSON ONE: INNOVATIONS AND FUTURE DIRECTIONS IN RESPIRATORY CARE

The field of respiratory care is constantly evolving with advancements in technology, research, and clinical practices. This lesson explores the latest innovations and future directions in respiratory care, highlighting the potential for improved patient outcomes and enhanced quality of care.

TECHNOLOGICAL ADVANCEMENTS

Telemedicine and Remote Monitoring:

- Telemedicine: The use of telehealth platforms to provide remote consultations, monitor patients, and manage chronic respiratory conditions. This approach enhances access to care, especially for patients in remote or underserved areas.
- Remote Monitoring Devices: Wearable devices and home monitoring systems that track respiratory parameters such as oxygen saturation, respiratory rate, and lung function, allowing for early detection of exacerbations and timely interventions.

Artificial Intelligence (AI) and Machine Learning:

- Predictive Analytics: AI algorithms that analyze large datasets to predict patient outcomes, identify high-risk patients, and guide clinical decision-making. These tools can help in anticipating respiratory crises and optimizing treatment plans.

- Automated Diagnostics: AI-powered systems that assist in interpreting diagnostic tests such as spirometry, radiographs, and CT scans, improving diagnostic accuracy and efficiency.

Advanced Ventilation Techniques:

- High-Frequency Ventilation: Newer modes of mechanical ventilation, such as high-frequency oscillatory ventilation (HFOV), that provide effective respiratory support with lower risk of lung injury.
- Adaptive Support Ventilation (ASV): Intelligent ventilation modes that automatically adjust ventilator settings based on the patient's respiratory mechanics and needs, optimizing ventilation and reducing the risk of complications.

INNOVATIONS IN TREATMENT MODALITIES

Personalized Medicine:

- Genomic Medicine: Utilizing genetic information to tailor treatments for respiratory diseases such as asthma, cystic fibrosis, and chronic obstructive pulmonary disease (COPD). This approach aims to improve treatment efficacy and minimize adverse effects.
- Biologics and Targeted Therapies: Development of biologic drugs that target specific pathways involved in respiratory diseases, offering more effective treatment options for conditions like severe asthma and idiopathic pulmonary fibrosis.

Regenerative Medicine and Stem Cell Therapy:

- Lung Regeneration: Research into stem cell therapy and tissue engineering to repair or regenerate damaged lung tissue. These therapies hold promise for treating chronic lung diseases and reducing the need for lung transplantation.
- Ex Vivo Lung Perfusion (EVLP): Techniques to improve the viability of donor lungs for transplantation by treating and assessing them outside the body before transplantation.

Enhanced Drug Delivery Systems:

- Inhaler Technology: Innovations in inhaler design, such as smart inhalers that track usage and provide feedback to patients and healthcare providers, improving adherence and treatment outcomes.
- Nebulization Techniques: Advances in nebulizer technology that enhance the delivery of medications to the lungs, improving the efficiency and effectiveness of respiratory treatments.

RESEARCH AND EVIDENCE-BASED PRACTICE

Clinical Trials and Research Studies:

- Ongoing Research: Participation in and application of findings from clinical trials and research studies to continually update and improve respiratory care practices.
- Translational Research: Bridging the gap between laboratory research and clinical practice to bring innovative treatments and technologies to patients more quickly.

Guidelines and Protocols:

- Evidence-Based Guidelines: Development and implementation of guidelines based on the latest research to standardize and improve the quality of respiratory care.
- Protocol-Driven Care: Utilizing protocols and care pathways to ensure consistent and effective management of respiratory conditions, reducing variability in care and improving outcomes.

FUTURE DIRECTIONS

Integrative and Holistic Approaches:

- Holistic Care Models: Integrating respiratory care with other aspects of health and well-being, such as nutrition, mental health, and physical therapy, to provide comprehensive and patient-centered care.

- Patient Engagement: Empowering patients to take an active role in their care through education, self-management programs, and shared decision-making.

Global Health Initiatives:

- Addressing Health Disparities: Implementing strategies to reduce health disparities and improve access to respiratory care in low-resource settings and underserved populations.
- Global Collaboration: Collaborating with international organizations and healthcare providers to share knowledge, resources, and best practices in respiratory care.

Sustainable Practices:

- Environmental Impact: Addressing the environmental impact of respiratory care practices, such as the use of inhalers and medical gases, and promoting sustainable practices in healthcare.
- Green Technologies: Developing and implementing environmentally friendly technologies and practices in respiratory care to reduce the carbon footprint and promote sustainability.

The future of respiratory care is bright, with numerous innovations and advancements poised to transform the field. By embracing technological advancements, personalized medicine, regenerative therapies, and evidence-based practices, healthcare providers can enhance the quality of care and improve patient outcomes. Integrative approaches, global health initiatives, and sustainable practices will further contribute to a holistic and forward-thinking approach to respiratory care.

DISCUSSION QUESTIONS

- What are the key legal requirements related to informed consent, confidentiality, and the scope of practice in respiratory care, and how can providers ensure they are compliant with these regulations?

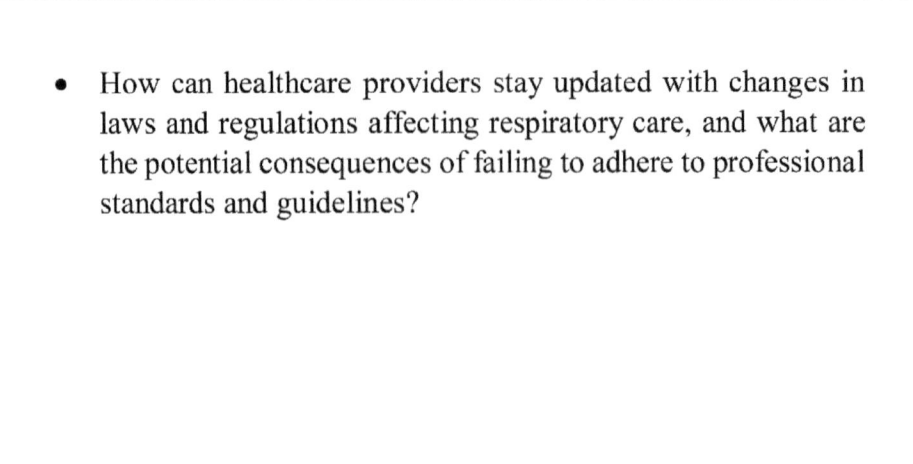

- How can healthcare providers stay updated with changes in laws and regulations affecting respiratory care, and what are the potential consequences of failing to adhere to professional standards and guidelines?

CONCLUSION

The field of respiratory care is critical to the well-being of patients with respiratory conditions, ranging from acute emergencies to chronic diseases. By emphasizing quality and safety, healthcare providers can significantly improve patient outcomes and enhance the overall standard of care. Understanding the fundamentals of respiratory physiology, conducting thorough assessments, and utilizing advanced diagnostic tools are essential for accurate diagnosis and effective treatment. Therapeutic interventions, both invasive and non-invasive, must be carefully selected and implemented to balance benefits and risks while ensuring patient adherence through education and involvement.

The pursuit of excellence in respiratory care quality and safety demands a multifaceted approach. This includes a deep understanding of respiratory physiology, meticulous patient assessment and monitoring, effective therapeutic interventions, rigorous infection control measures, continuous quality improvement efforts, and the integration of advanced technologies. Additionally, addressing the unique needs of special populations and adhering to ethical and legal standards are crucial to providing comprehensive and equitable respiratory care. By fostering a culture of safety, continuous improvement, and patient-centered care, healthcare providers can significantly enhance the outcomes and quality of life for patients with respiratory conditions.

REFERENCES

American Thoracic Society. (2013). *Guidelines for the Management of Adults with Hospital-acquired, Ventilator-associated, and Healthcare-associated Pneumonia. American Journal of Respiratory and Critical Care Medicine.*

Bakke, P., & Gulsvik, A. (2000). *Preventive Strategies for Chronic Respiratory Diseases. European Respiratory Journal.*

Barrett, A. J., & Malek, J. (2019). *Ethical Challenges in Respiratory Care. Journal of Clinical Ethics.*

Celli, B. R., & MacNee, W. (2004). *Standards for the Diagnosis and Treatment of Patients with COPD: A Summary of the ATS/ERS Position Paper. European Respiratory Journal.*

Egan, D. F., & Davies, R. (2015). *Mechanical Ventilation: Clinical Applications and Current Practices. Critical Care Clinics.*

Gosselink, R., & Langer, D. (2018). *Pulmonary Rehabilitation for Patients with Respiratory Diseases. Respiratory Care.*

Hogg, J. C., & Timens, W. (2009). *The Pathology of Chronic Obstructive Pulmonary Disease. Annual Review of Pathology: Mechanisms of Disease.*

Kallet, R. H., & Branson, R. D. (2017). *Respiratory Care Protocols: An Evidence-Based Approach. Respiratory Care.*

Milton Keynes UK
Ingram Content Group UK Ltd.
UKHW050309140724
445568UK00009B/54